Doña Gracia's Secret
The Adventures of an Extraordinary Jewish Woman in the Renaissance

Marilyn Froggatt

gefen גפן
publishing house בית הוצאה לאור
JERUSALEM ◆ NEW YORK   Est. 1981

Copyright © Marilyn Froggatt
Jerusalem 2020/5780

Cover Design: Optume Technologies
Typesetting: Optume Technologies
Map: Cartographer Daniel Spring, San Francisco

ISBN: 978-965-7023-08-2

1 3 5 7 9 8 6 4 2

Gefen Publishing House Ltd.
6 Hatzvi Street
Jerusalem 9438614,
Israel
972-2-538-0247
orders@gefenpublishing.com

Gefen Books
c/o 3PL Center,
3003 Woodbridge Ave.
Edison, NJ 08837
516-593-1234
orders@gefenpublishing.com

www.gefenpublishing.com

Printed in Israel
Library of Congress Cataloging-in-Publication Data

Names: Froggatt, Marilyn, author.
Title: Dona Gracia's Secret : the adventures of an extraordinary Jewish
    woman in the Renaissance / by Marilyn Froggatt.
Description: New Jersey ; Jerusalem : Gefen Books, [2019]
Identifiers: LCCN 2019010199 | ISBN 9789657023082
Subjects: LCSH: Nasi, Gracia, approximately 1510-1569--Juvenile literature. |
    Jewish women--Portugal--Biography--Juvenile literature. |
    Sephardim--Portugal--Biography--Juvenile literature. |
    Marranos--Portugal--Biography--Juvenile literature. | Jewish
    women--Turkey--Biography--Juvenile literature.
Classification: LCC DS135.P8 N3735 2019 | DDC 946.9/004924/0092--
dc23 LC record available at https://lccn.loc.gov/2019010199

This book is dedicated to my late parents,
Charles and Anne Studnitz,
and to my late husband, Gordon Froggatt.
They left this world far too soon.
Thank you for your everlasting love.

Long ago and far away lived a real-life hero: Doña Gracia Mendes Nasi, who knew how to keep a secret. Totally committed to what she believed in, she never gave up.

I hope that Doña Gracia's remarkable story will inspire young women everywhere to become authors of their own lives.

M. F.

Toronto, 2019

CONTENTS

ONCE UPON A SECRET

This is the story of an amazing hero who worked wonders to follow her dream, one of the most famous women in the world in her day, who was nearly forgotten for five hundred years.

Gracia was born into a prominent Sephardic[1] Jewish family in Lisbon, Portugal, in 1510 but baptized as a Christian. Why? Because life at that time was very dangerous for anyone who didn't practice the Catholic faith.

Until she died in 1569, Gracia's life was a roller-coaster ride.

Even before she was born, religious persecution meant that her family had to escape from Spain to Portugal just to stay alive. Then they had to pretend to be Christians while secretly practicing Judaism – knowing that if they were caught, they might be tortured and burned at the stake.

A bride at eighteen, Gracia would all too soon become a widow, feeling helpless and wondering what would happen next in the life she now shared only with her little daughter Ana and her younger sister Brianda. Yet just a few years later, in an era when such success was nearly impossible for women, Gracia had

---

[1] Sephardic Jews are Jews from Spain. It is estimated that 200,000 of them were exiled from that country in 1492. Their name comes from the word *Sefarad*, which is Hebrew for Spain.

become a mega business tycoon in the international spice trade,[2] precious stones market, and banking.

By then, she was so strategically savvy and socially well connected that she managed to minimize persecution by an all-powerful pope of a group of secret Jews like herself. Her strategy was to arrange a financial maneuver that brought business in a key Mediterranean port to a screeching halt.

As if all that weren't bold enough to earn her a special place in history, Gracia maintained what today we would call an underground railroad to help Jews escape to safety. Doing so, while also keeping herself and her family safe from the murderous, heretic-seeking Inquisition,[3] led to hair-raising escapes from country to country – one step ahead of threatening popes, queens, and high officials who coveted her wealth. It was a dangerous game of hide and seek in which the stakes were human lives – her own, her family's, and those of countless other secret Jews.

---

[2]   In its day, the spice trade was one of the world's largest industries. The sources of its products were tightly guarded and offered tremendous riches to those who discovered and managed them. Trying to reach the areas where spices were grown, rather than dealing with authorities in Venice, was almost an obsession of every sixteenth-century spice trader. Lisbon was considered the best trade port for spices en route to Europe. But dealing with the port was extremely costly, since Venice added tariffs to the shipments. Then, in 1497, a Portuguese man named Vasco da Gama navigated four vessels around the Cape of Good Hope and managed to reach India, the mecca for spices of all kinds. This triumph proved to be a gateway to many Asian growers and was said to be the birth of the Portuguese empire. It also increased the fortunes of the Mendes companies.

[3]   The Spanish Inquisition was a Catholic tribunal that began in Spain in the fifteenth century and then moved to other countries. Its purpose was to discover, punish, and eliminate heresy (non-Catholic beliefs). The Inquisition's methods involved terrorizing, brutal questioning without a defense lawyer or any sort of protection for the accused, and severe punishments, the ultimate of which was death by fire.

Above all, Doña Gracia made her most cherished dream come true, for herself and for many, many others. That dream is embedded in the hearts of Jews everywhere: the longing to return to the Promised Land from which they were exiled thousands of years ago.

Here's how Doña Gracia's exciting life story began.

The World
of
Doña Gracia

A map showing the documented travels of
Doña Gracia in the 16th century

EUROPE

ENGLAND
London

FRANCE
Paris

HOLY ROMAN EMPIRE

ALPS

Vienna
BUDA

Antwerp
1536–1544

Venice 1544–1549
VENETIAN REPUBLIC
Ferrara
1549–1552
Ancona
1555
PAPAL STATES
Rome
NAPLES
Naples

OTTOMAN EMPIRE

Ragusa
(Dubrovnik)
Salonika

BLACK SEA

Constantinople
1553–1569

Athens

MEDITERRANEAN SEA

AFRICA

SPAIN
Madrid
Seville

PORTUGAL

Lisbon
1510–1536

ATLANTIC OCEAN

Tiberias
Jerusalem
Cairo

0   100 200 400   600   800 1,000 Miles

ONE

LOVE AND LOSS IN LISBON

When she was a teenager, Doña Gracia Nasi faced her first tragedy: the death of her parents. Becoming an orphan at such a young age was bitterly painful. And she didn't know who to turn to for comfort or advice. Not her older brother Samuel, a doctor, always busy and whom she rarely saw. Certainly not her sister Brianda who, like most girls her age, was only interested in her social life. By contrast, Gracia was more serious and thoughtful and interested in what was happening in the wider world.

One day not long before her parents died, Gracia's life changed completely when her mother sat her down for an important talk. "Even though our family has always lived as 'New Christians,'[4] and we were baptized as Catholics after being expelled from Spain and moving to Portugal," she told her astonished daughter, "we are actually secret Jews."

Her mother then expressed her dearest wish: that Gracia honor her true birthright by finding a way to live a Jewish life despite the necessity of pretending to be Christian.

Gracia was shaken by what her mother said. Until then, she had lived as an observant Catholic, faithfully attending Mass and

---

[4] "New Christians" were Jews who had officially converted by being baptized and changing their names.

practicing church rituals in a magnificent Catholic cathedral in Lisbon.

Her family were famous as wealthy and influential members of the New Christian community. They were highly respected and involved in many of its causes and charities. Gracia wasn't the only one who had never suspected that their Catholicism might be a disguise.

She *had* known about a group of poor Portuguese Jews who claimed to have publicly converted to Catholicism but were suspected of practicing Judaism in secret. Known in Spanish as *conversos*[5] and in Hebrew as *anusim* (converted ones), and mocked as *marranos* (Spanish for "pigs"), these people had lived in constant fear of exposure because they had avoided being baptized as Christians. They faced extreme scrutiny and possible arrest unless they could afford to bribe officials to protect them. Every waking moment, they knew that if their Judaism were discovered, they would face torture and probably death.

When Gracia learned that her parents wanted her to live as a Jew while keeping her heritage hidden, she vowed to try to honor their wishes despite the danger.

Gracia resolved to take the first step by learning what being Jewish really meant. But she soon realized that delving into the heart of the ancient religion would not be easy even though as a child, she had unknowingly observed Jewish customs her family took care to conceal – such as fasting on traditional Jewish fast days and not eating pork.

At the time of Gracia's birth, observing Judaism was forbidden in Portugal. This meant that synagogues were closed, and there were no practicing rabbis. The result was that the religious beliefs

---

[5]   "Conversos" were Jews who claimed to have converted to Christianity but were only pretending for their own safety. For the same reason, they often changed their names. These Jews were the main target of the Inquisition.

2

and rituals secret Jews performed were sometimes based merely on oral history handed down by elders or just customs that were special to individual families.

While grappling with these confusing obstacles, Gracia learned another surprising truth. Her aunt Rachel, while pretending to be a New Christian, had a secret synagogue in her home. Hidden in the basement, the small space held remnants of the faith in ancient Hebrew prayer books. Now Gracia could begin learning what she yearned to know about Judaism and have a safe place to pray.

As time passed, she became more and more intrigued with the religion she had known so little about. But she was wise enough to keep her new knowledge to herself. These were tumultuous times, and Gracia knew she had to be on guard to protect herself and the rest of her household. She couldn't even tell her sister Brianda about their parents' true faith because she was too young to keep such a crucial secret.

Even though she was excited by all she was learning about her heritage, Gracia was also coming to understand the fragility of life at a time when the barbaric Inquisition was expected to spread from Spain to her home in Portugal. Its intent, as always, was to wipe out all practicing Jews.

"Who can I trust to help me learn more about my birthright?" she wondered. Her aunt suggested seeking assistance from another New Christian.

His name was Señor Francisco Mendes, a kind and wise family friend and relative. He was a very wealthy, highly respected trader of spices and other in-demand goods. Francisco was also a financier to kings and popes and other VIPs across Europe who depended upon him for large loans. These clients included Emperor Charles V of the Holy Roman Empire, King Henry VIII of England, and King John of Portugal.

If any of these clients suspected that their banker was a secret Jew, they kept quiet about it to keep vast sums of money flowing into their bank accounts. Another closely guarded secret was that Francisco was giving money to conversos to help them stay safe until they could flee persecution. To make escape possible, he was financing and operating a spy network with many of his own employees acting as secret agents.

Gracia instinctively recognized that in Francisco, she had found the trustworthy mentor she needed. Yet he tried to dissuade her from studying. Why? Because he was living in a time when females were considered incapable of scholarly pursuits. But when he saw how intelligent and determined she was, he changed his attitude.

They began meeting once a week, and as the student-teacher relationship developed, Gracia proved to be a quick learner. Francisco was an excellent, patient teacher who always smiled as he listened to her increasingly fluent and deeply emotional reading of Hebrew prayers. Learning them was a challenge because they were written in Hebrew, which uses a completely different alphabet and is read from right to left, unlike Spanish, Portuguese, and many other languages.

Francisco's approval boosted Gracia's self-confidence. Even so, she was saddened by the necessity of having to conceal Sabbath rituals, such as lighting candles on Friday night, in a dark room with tightly covered windows to avoid discovery.

Along with Gracia's joy in exploring her religion was a sense of foreboding. She kept having nightmares about Inquisitors violently sweeping through the narrow Portuguese streets, carrying flickering torches, hoping to hunt down Jews and set them ablaze.

Although Francisco was considerably older than Gracia, she thought he was very handsome. And she was never happier than when looking into his warm brown eyes.

Francisco was impressed with her. She was impressed with him. So impressed that in spite of the age difference, they gradually realized that they wanted to marry.

In sixteenth-century Portugal, Jewish marriages were arranged – sometimes at birth – by the parents of brides and grooms to cement ties between wealthy, influential families. Marrying her mother's wealthy relative was considered an excellent match for Gracia.

And by becoming the wife of her devout and prominent mentor, Gracia would fulfill her mother's wishes. Together they could lead a truly Jewish life while posing as Catholics.

Royal consent to the marriage of someone as important as Francisco was a necessity, so Francisco took Gracia to meet King John. Impressed by her grace and sophistication and clueless about the couple being Jewish, he gave their union his official seal of approval.

Gracia's marriage at eighteen, conducted in the grand Cathedral of Lisbon, was lavish and moving and observed all the appropriate Catholic traditions. In attendance, dressed in their most elegant finery, were the king and many important members of Portuguese and European society.

No one in the cathedral that day knew that Gracia and Francisco had already consecrated their marriage. Early that morning, they had performed a secret Jewish ceremony and signed the traditional wedding contract, called a ketubah.

Gracia's happy life with her new husband was enriched when the couple had a daughter they named Ana. The family's lifestyle was extravagant thanks to the prosperity of the House of Mendes business, which Francisco owned with his younger brother, Diogo Mendes, whose headquarters was in Belgium.

But eight years into the union, Gracia faced another tragedy. Her husband suddenly died, shattering her world once again.

At twenty-six, she was a widow – but a very wealthy widow, because Francisco had defied all contemporary traditions by bequeathing his half of the lucrative House of Mendes to her.

That fortune, along with the substantial money she had inherited from her parents, made Gracia a woman of enormous wealth – said to be in the millions – wealth she knew she would need to protect her family from the Inquisition.

TWO

HOUSE OF MENDES –
BUILDING A NEW LIFE

When Francisco died so suddenly, Gracia's world turned upside down once again. Ever since her parents' deaths, she had relied solely on her husband for support, not only in raising their daughter but also in handling the tricky reality of everyday life.

That reality had included publicly posing as a Catholic while secretly practicing her true faith. All the while, she and her husband had used their wealth on behalf of conversos, sending them money for food and shelter and to bribe officials to ignore their presence.

Gracia was still reeling from the shock of her husband's death when she heard some terrifying news. A group of savage Inquisitors was on its way to Portugal – on orders from the pope – to wipe out all the secret Jews they could find.

Imagine the timing.

It seemed that Gracia's terrifying nightmares might be coming true. Not only were her family and friends now in imminent danger, the Inquisitors were also blazing a trail to the conversos' homes.

"What should I do?" she agonized.

The answer came in one of the conversations she was still having with Francisco in her dreams. One decisive night, his deep voice, imprinted in her memory, urged her to escape to a safer place as quickly as possible.

She took his warning to heart and immediately began preparing for a sea voyage to Antwerp, Belgium, where her husband's brother Diogo was operating the headquarters of the Mendes conglomerate. He had been urging her to escape for weeks.

Gracia knew she had to pack up with as little fuss as possible to avoid unwanted attention. This included covertly preparing one of the company's spice ships for the voyage, putting many of her furnishings and valuables into storage, and stocking the ship's kitchens with food and emergency provisions.

A ship was soon readied to sustain Gracia's family for weeks on end during which they might face unpredictable seas, sudden illness, and even vicious pirates.

When everything was ready, Gracia, along with her daughter Ana, her sister Brianda, her two young nephews Joseph and Samuel (children of her brother Samuel), and her beloved housekeeper sneaked out of Lisbon in the early hours of the morning.

In the harbor, she looked back at the city of her birth, shuddered, and uttered a deep sigh of relief. But her face glistened with tears.

Then a wide smile began spreading over her features. She instinctively knew that she was leaving behind a life that would soon exist only in her memory. But her beloved mentor was coming along – if only in her imagination.

"Thank you again, Francisco, for being my husband and still taking care of us in these dangerous times," she said ever so softly. "We are leaving behind a climate of fear and heading toward a new life, one with hope."

You could say that this was the exact moment when Gracia's own story was set in motion, to begin in earnest in distant Antwerp.

THREE

A WOMAN AHEAD OF HER TIME

W hen Gracia spotted her brother-in-law Diogo on the wharf in Antwerp, she began to relax. He was much younger than his deceased brother, but the family resemblance was striking. His smile, so like Francisco's, put her at ease.

And when Diogo took the family on a tour of Antwerp, they were impressed by its beauty. They were also excited by all he had done to ensure that they would be happy in their new home, as well as safe from the Inquisition.

Diogo had turned part of the large, handsome property – which symbolized the House of Mendes wealth and international prominence – into a spacious, light-filled apartment tastefully furnished with a large selection of paintings.

Brianda began learning Flemish, the language of the northern part of Belgium, with Diogo's help. And Ana explored her new home during exciting horseback rides around the city with her cousins Joseph and Samuel.

Here in Antwerp, Gracia felt it was time to return to her baptismal name, Beatriz.[6]

---

[6]   For their own safety, conversos and New Christians like Doña Gracia took at least two names throughout their lives. For Gracia, it was multiple names as her circumstances changed. When she was born in Portugal, her baptismal name

As the days and months passed, Beatriz spent most of her time with Diogo, learning about the Mendes commercial activities. She had made a head start on this during her marriage, when she was part of Francisco's international world of trade and financing, often accompanying him to meetings with important clients.

As Diogo's new partner, Beatriz modeled her dealings with popes and kings and queens after the skilled and ethical way Francisco had conducted his transactions. Just as she had decided to honor her parents' wishes many years earlier, she was now determined to abide by her late husband's principles.

Before long, Beatriz had made a name for herself and a reputation as a very smart and powerful businesswoman. Expanding company operations to include luxury goods such as silk was just one of the innovations she is believed to have introduced. Another was marketing wool products, which became so desirable that the House of Mendes was later chosen to supply uniforms for the Ottoman army.

While Beatriz was at the helm of the company with Diogo, its global banking operations grew to become the second largest in the world. The conglomerate also built and acquired so many ships that it soon owned the largest private fleet in the world.

Meanwhile, her nephew Joseph was becoming her right-hand man, traveling through Europe representing Mendes interests and achieving one success after another.

Remember, this was all happening in sixteenth-century Europe, where few if any Renaissance women knew anything

---

(continued) was Beatriz de Luna. The parents who chose their daughter's name were Jews who had been exiled from Spain in 1497 and forcibly converted to Christianity in Portugal. But they only pretended to have renounced Judaism. When she married, Beatriz became Doña Gracia Mendes (*doña* is a Spanish honorific signifying a woman of noble or distinguished lineage). Nasi was her father's last name, which she used growing up and later in Ferrara, when she became known as Doña Gracia Mendes Nasi, the name she also used in Turkey.

about business – let alone had the expertise to run a firm the size and scope of the Mendes financial empire. Most women of the era were illiterate, and womanhood was defined solely by marriage and motherhood. Only a handful of women in royal families and wealthy dynasties – or widows in family ventures – held positions anywhere near as powerful as Beatriz's.

She was introducing a different kind of female – a daring and clever businesswoman whose connections embraced the world. She was also seeing to it that her daughter Ana was getting an education that would pave her way to becoming an independent woman when she grew up.

Wherever Beatriz went, she was entertained by kings and queens, dukes and duchesses who were intent on remaining in her favor. She sensed, beneath their surface hospitality, a secret desire to share in her wealth.

Queen Mary of Hungary, sister of Holy Roman Emperor King Charles V – who had depended for years on financing from Mendes banks – came up with a plan to tap into Mendes money. She would arrange a marriage between Beatriz and a member of the royal family. Beatriz somehow avoided this catastrophe, but there is no record of how she did it.

Meanwhile, Brianda's life also changed dramatically in Antwerp. She and Diogo fell in love, married, and had a daughter. But Brianda's world collapsed not long afterward, when he died, just as unexpectedly as his brother had.

Beatriz was now the boss of the entire Mendes empire.

Diogo left his half of the business equally to his wife and daughter, but named Beatriz administrator in charge of the fortune. This sparked a bitter feud when Brianda insisted upon receiving her inheritance directly. Beatriz refused because she feared that her impulsive sister would quickly squander the money.

FOUR

HIDE AND SEEK IN VENICE

T he next crisis arrived when Queen Mary, having failed to get her hands on the Mendes fortune before, now demanded that Ana marry a notoriously corrupt elderly Catholic nobleman.

Beatriz vowed that this would never happen. But avoiding the looming disaster soon brought the family to a crisis point. Suspecting that Queen Mary and King Charles would try to prevent her from leaving and taking her vast empire with her, she knew what she had to do. The only solution was to escape from Antwerp, which at that point was part of the Holy Roman Empire.

Beatriz decided to move to a safer city: Venice, Italy, which was an independent republic. There Ana could escape the powerful grasp of the royal court. And her mother could closely monitor what was happening to the conversos.

But more immediately pressing than these issues was the ever-present conflict between Brianda and Beatriz over Diogo's estate, which was still threatening their relationship.

Not long after the family arrived in Venice, Brianda, still insisting that she needed money immediately, decided to take inheritance matters into her own hands. Retaliating in the worst possible way, she denounced her sister to the authorities for being a secret Jew. Guards quickly arrived to arrest Beatriz and throw her into prison.

A few miserable days later, she was released – thanks only to skillful negotiating by her nephew Samuel and an enormous bribe to officials.

Shaken by her cruel treatment in prison and by the bitterness of the dispute with her sister, Beatriz finally gave in. She agreed to have the dispute settled by the Venetian tribunal that handled the affairs of foreigners.

After many months, a court decision was issued. Beatriz had won. But she decided to release her sister's money anyway. Soon afterward, she told Brianda that it was time for them to go their separate ways because their relationship was broken.

Apart from the problems with her sister, Beatriz had been enjoying her stay in Venice, where music, art, and books inspired her. Meanwhile, she dreamed of achieving a better future for the conversos.

A sparkling city built on water, Venice was at the center of international trade and drew people from all over the world. More importantly for Beatriz, the city was a relatively safe home for non-Christians. Jews had lived in Italy for over fifteen hundred years, ever since being forcibly taken from their Holy Land to be slaves in Rome.

In 1516, Venice became the site of the first Jewish ghetto when about two thousand Jews were confined to a small section of the city. It was walled off and gated, and only Jewish merchants and doctors – whose skills were essential to the economic and physical well-being of the city – were allowed to leave in daytime. In the evening, the gates were locked, and no one was allowed to leave.

Beatriz did not live in the ghetto, however. In Venice, she chose to continue behaving with her family as New Christians in public while practicing her true faith in private. Every waking moment, she was tip-toeing through life, conscious of what might happen if the secret of her real identity was revealed. Sometimes she would awaken at night shivering, remembering her harrowing stay in the Italian prison.

Beatriz felt that her grand lifestyle was a necessary ruse. As wealthy New Christians, her family had been given permission to reside on the Grand Canal, where she carried on her commercial business in plain sight while hiding her ongoing efforts to help the local conversos. Mendes bribes were still secretly going into the treasuries of religious officials to save the conversos, just as they had before the Inquisition landed in Portugal.

The stakes for the conversos were getting higher every day. While some of them had become successful in Antwerp, owning and operating merchant vessels, the majority were extremely poor. They had to wander from place to place, their belongings hidden under coats with precious possessions sewn into the lining.

Beatriz and her family had successfully escaped danger by fleeing to Antwerp and then to Venice. But now, with the Inquisition growing more relentless every day in Portugal, hundreds of conversos remained stranded there (as well as in Spain). Their chances of survival were slim unless they could escape quickly and find refuge somewhere else.

Beatriz began strategizing the details. First, she would revamp the escape routes she and Francisco had developed in Portugal to ensure safe passage on Mendes ships. Upon reaching Antwerp, the conversos would then cross the immense and treacherous Alps mountain range on foot to get to Venice. Only extreme desperation drove them to attempt this dangerous journey.

When all Beatriz's rescue plans were in place and the sky was dark, small boats quietly ferried conversos to Mendes ships docked in several ports. On board, some of the escapees were disguised as priests. Others were concealed among bolts of cloth and rolls of tapestries or stuffed into wooden barrels marked as cargo to keep them safe until they arrived in Antwerp.

Fortunately, before his death, Diogo had earmarked funds to continue enabling conversos to escape persecution. That meant money was available for the conversos to secretly flee to Antwerp, then on to Venice and ultimately beyond the grasp of the Inquisition to Constantinople (now called Istanbul), in the Ottoman Empire.[7]

---

[7] The Ottoman Empire, which stretched from the Middle Ages until the twentieth century when the last sultan was exiled, covered a vast swath of territory including countries in the Middle East, Baltics, and North Africa.

FIVE

FINDING HER JEWISH SELF

I n 1549, Beatriz and her daughter Ana moved from Venice to Ferrara, Italy. Jews had lived there for hundreds of years, and a strong Sephardic community was thriving.

Amazingly, Beatriz had had no idea how highly regarded she had become until arriving in Ferrara. Thanks to a whispering campaign in Jewish communities, her heroic rescue efforts were becoming legendary throughout Europe – even though her "underground railroad" had to be kept in the shadows to elude the authorities.

Beatriz was overwhelmed by what she heard in Ferrara. "*Shalom*" (hello), said a smiling rabbi to both mother and daughter. Astonished, Beatriz replied, "*Shalom*."

For the first time in her life, she was seeing her Jewish identity being openly acknowledged. Although taken by surprise, she cautiously began to feel she had truly found a safe place for herself and her daughter.

After months living in Ferrara, Beatriz felt comfortable enough to cast off her double life. Her first step was choosing to return to her Spanish name: Gracia.[8] For Ana, she chose a popular name for Jewish girls: Reyna.

---

[8] After escaping to Ferrara, Italy, she felt safe to assume her Jewish identity while still pretending to be a New Christian. At home, Beatriz was known as Gracia –

Gracia, as a secret Jew, had never before been free to openly practise her religion or share her faith with other Jews (except Francisco), but now she was about to.

On a bright, sunny spring morning when the sun had barely risen, she entered Ferrara's ancient Sephardic synagogue and heard the soft murmur of voices breaking the silence. Gracia remembered that this was the time in the week reserved only for women congregants, when they could meet to sing, study Hebrew texts, and have lively discussions about their religion together.

Suddenly, a strong female voice began singing a Hebrew prayer, beautifully and with deep emotion. Next, a young woman read a holy text. When she finished, others in the group began to discuss what the words meant to them.

Gracia's face became flushed. As she felt color rising in her cheeks, Francisco's face appeared to her. Once again, she heard him speaking gently to her, just as he had many years ago when she was just a young woman in Portugal learning about her true faith.

"Ah, Gracia," he whispered, "remember when we used to read a passage together, how awed we were to share the experience? What you're seeing here today is what our religion is all about."

Instinctively she knew what Francisco meant. Together they had sensed a deep feeling of belonging to each other, but also a strong sense of community and a faith far greater than themselves.

When the singer in the group saw the newcomer standing alone, she invited her to join them. Elated, Gracia did so. This experience was Gracia's true spiritual awakening.

(continued) the equivalent of the Hebrew name Hannah. When she found true safety in Constantinople, she became publicly known as Doña Gracia.

This experience was also Gracia's true intellectual awakening. From that moment on, she passed her time in Ferrara busily exploring her place in the community and hosting get-togethers with her new friends to discuss books, art, and Jewish history.

She worshipped in the synagogue, took part in countless study groups, and donated money for the publication of the *Ferrara Bible.* It was dedicated to Gracia and written in the Ladino language, a melding of Hebrew and Spanish that was spoken at the time by Sephardic Jews.

Then one night her nephew Joseph, now the top agent for the Mendes conglomerate, arrived in Ferrara. Like his aunt, he had become legendary throughout Europe, where his trading and negotiating skills were highly respected.

After many tears and hugs, Joseph, who was now a dashingly handsome young man, said that he had great news he knew Gracia had been longing to hear. He gently led her outside to the large terrace at the back of the villa and asked her to sit down.

Excitedly, Joseph said, "The leader of the Ottoman Empire, Sultan Suleiman I the Magnificent, has agreed to welcome you, and the Mendes family and business, to live freely as Jews in Constantinople. He asked me to extend an invitation to you and to our people to come to his land and settle there as soon as possible."

Joseph explained that even though Suleiman was a Muslim, he had no problem inviting Jews to live and work in his empire, "because he feels we will bring further prosperity. Therefore," Joseph added, "Jews will be granted residency and freedom to live, worship, and work in the sultan's country in exchange for paying an entrance tax."

He looked at Gracia, whose eyes were sparkling like the stars above them. She started to clap her hands, crying "Bravo!" over and over again.

Later, departing from Salonika, Greece, on her way to Constantinople, Gracia felt like pinching herself. She could hardly believe she had finally found a safe haven for her family, her business and, of course, her beloved conversos.

Gracia's arrival in Constantinople was a triumphant pageant. With her – in four coaches laden with trunks full of glittering valuables – were her daughter Reyna and an enormous entourage of servants. Prancing alongside were forty horses bearing the sultan's colorfully clad private guards who had guarded them on their arduous journey.

The magnificent spectacle caused a sensation even more exciting than when famous celebrities make big entrances today. Bells were ringing. Masses of people were singing and clapping. A crowd of Ottoman artists, performers, and musicians paraded through the streets wearing extravagant costumes. They serenaded the newcomers and praised Gracia as "the Queen of the Jews" all the way to the sultan's majestic palace.

Though Gracia hadn't known it, Suleiman had been monitoring her activities from afar for years. He was extremely impressed by everything he had learned about her.

Gracia had contacted the sultan to ask for advice about preparing documents, signing agreements, and drafting contracts in his country while planning her departure from Ferrara. As head of one of the most powerful companies in Europe, she had absorbed all the finer points of running a business. Now she was determined to use every means possible to maintain an equivalent position in Constantinople.

Escorted into the sultan's private chambers, Gracia was impressed with the spectacular opulence. Suleiman, wearing a luxurious silk robe and turban, was quite a sight as he warmly greeted her.

We may never know what they talked about or in which language. But for Gracia, it seems to have been a successful meeting. She had prepared well and knew what she wanted to say. As for the sultan, he recognized that a very special, courageous woman was seated in front of him.

Gracia was only in her early forties when she arrived in Constantinople and had many productive years ahead of her. She had sailed through life on Mendes vessels for seventeen years, living at risk as a secret Jew yet keeping strong control of her vast empire.

The breadth of her travels was astounding. At a time when cars and trains and planes were unimaginable, long journeys were rough and dangerous. Yet she managed to make it through England, Belgium, the Netherlands, France, Italy, Ragusa (today the Croatian city of Dubrovnik), Greece, and much more, covering at least three thousand miles.

En route, she was always on guard against possible perils or betrayal by her enemies who, jealous of her great wealth, could have denounced her to the Inquisition at any time. Her fortune allowed her to avoid personal attacks by always keeping security guards nearby.

Undoubtedly, Gracia's status and history of defying royalty and popes to save her people were important factors in Suleiman's decision to help her and the conversos.

Gracia knew that the sultan was powerful enough to open doors for her and help her deal with issues she considered extremely important. She was ready and anxious to get started.

SIX

THE PROMISE - GRACIA, JOSEPH, AND THE SULTAN

While her family was happily settling into a luxurious estate called Belvedere in the European quarter of Constantinople, Gracia dealt with a matter that had been haunting her ever since Diogo's death.

Aside from simply saving the conversos' lives, Gracia now felt a deep responsibility for their spiritual well-being in their new homeland. Few of them had been formally schooled in the basics of Judaism because synagogues and Hebrew texts had been banned in Portugal, before and during the Inquisition. Now their religious education was about to begin – ironically in a Muslim country.

Although synagogues had long existed in Turkey, Gracia had a vision of building a handsome new one in Izmir on the Aegean Sea. Her aim was to establish a secure community of their own for the conversos – to keep their Jewish identity alive in their hearts and in their homes.

With the sultan's support, a synagogue named La Senora (The Lady) was built and dedicated in Gracia's honor. Nearby, there was to be a school where converso children could learn Hebrew so they could read prayers.

Gracia also built other synagogues throughout the Ottoman Empire. One of them was in Salonika, where a large Jewish population had lived for centuries, and wealthier Portuguese conversos had formed their own congregation. Amazingly, some of these places of worship still exist today.

During her first year in Constantinople, Gracia felt contented. Her family was no longer on the move, and she had begun to think of the city as her home, her anchor.

Days were filled with Mendes business obligations plus her many charitable duties. In the evenings, she often entertained rich and powerful guests from Western Europe and the Ottoman Empire. Sometimes there were as many as eighty at her beautifully decorated table. Elsewhere and with the same graciousness, she fed the poor and needy.

This was also the time when she felt ready to fulfill the promise she had made to her mother and her husband. She would have their remains disinterred from Lisbon cemeteries and taken for reburial in one of Jerusalem's holy cemeteries.

A year after Gracia and her family had settled in, her nephew Joseph entered Constantinople on horseback with twenty servants following behind him. His enthusiastic reception rivaled her own. It was obvious that he had grown in status to become a person of great wealth and connections, particularly with European royalty and of course the sultan.

Besides being an extremely valuable part of the Mendes conglomerate, Joseph had helped Gracia personally in many ways. The most dramatic instance was when he arranged for her and her daughter Ana to escape to Venice to avoid Queen Mary's greedy marriage scheme. And it was Joseph who had negotiated the return of family possessions from Antwerp after King Charles and his sister Mary seized them. Now he would soon take on another, more personal role.

At last secure in Constantinople, Gracia was ready to honor another promise she had made to Francisco before his death. It was to arrange the marriage of Ana to a suitable husband.

Joseph seemed the perfect candidate. Gracia knew that their marriage, following the practice of wealthy Jews marrying each other, would have met with Francisco's approval.

The wedding was the Mendes family's first major celebration in their new home. As a bonus to Gracia's happiness, she and her sister Brianda had by now reconciled their past disagreements and renewed their relationship.

What the guests enjoyed that day was a traditional Jewish ceremony, conducted under a ritual *chuppah* (canopy) with a rabbi officiating and then the signing of the ketubah.

Reyna was a dazzling vision in a bridal gown fashioned from the finest silks and luxury fabrics imported from the Mendes French collection.

As the couple stood under the *chuppah*, Gracia imagined her mother at her side, clasping her hand and saying, "Thank you, my daughter, for honoring my request when you were so young and unaware of the dangers of carrying out my wish that you secretly lead a Jewish life any way you could."

Reyna and Joseph's marriage ceremony was witnessed by hundreds of residents of Constantinople, from Portuguese conversos who had never been to a Jewish wedding before to Jews from Salonika whose knowledge of Jewish rituals was historical.

When she heard the traditional shattering of glass under the groom's foot – along with a joyful burst of voices shouting "*Mazal tov*," the customary expression of congratulations, this was surely one of the sweetest and proudest moments in Gracia's life.

But her happiness would soon be overshadowed by yet another wave of despair when she heard of disturbing news unfolding in the Italian sea port of Ancona.

SEVEN

THE INQUISITION -
TAKING A STAND

I t was one of Constantinople's hottest days when Gracia received some horrifying reports. A large group of Portuguese conversos – among them an employee of the House of Mendes – were to be burned at the stake in Ancona on orders from the pope.

Gracia was in shock. She knew that the newly installed Pope Paul IV had a reputation for being harsh and unyielding and that he was determined to bring about many changes.

He was now in charge of Ancona, an important Italian port in the Mediterranean with vital commercial ties to the East. Records reveal that Jews had lived in this area since the tenth century. The presence of a Jewish community was tolerated, although not necessarily encouraged. There had been a time when Jews were forced to live on a single street and wear badges identifying their religion.

Then, when Ancona became part of the Papal States in 1429, many powerful forces recognized a tremendous commercial opportunity. They transformed the city into a booming financial hub operating as a free port and a gateway to eastern markets. This burst of commercial activity had resulted in a more favorable attitude toward the approximately two thousand Jews who had settled into the community long ago, as well as toward the Portuguese conversos, who had fled the Inquisition and later migrated to Ancona.

The papacy had long valued the advantage of working with Jews, whose expertise in banking and moneylending was legendary. Jewish businessmen had become a valuable asset to any commercial sector.

But as Ancona's Jewish population gradually expanded, the demographics of the town changed. Jews who had lived there, often for centuries, were at odds with the conversos – who now considered the port their home but didn't always see eye to eye with the original Jewish settlers.

Pope Paul IV, now governing the state, was definitely not pro-Jewish, and soon his main target was primarily the conversos. He expressed his beliefs in a papal bull (an edict or decree) in 1555. Its purpose was to force a choice on them: become Christians by baptism or face death.

Gracia recognized the significance of the wording in the bull as soon as she read it. These were the same hateful words of the dreaded Inquisition, which had forced her and her family to escape from Portugal years earlier.

She immediately contacted the sultan. He agreed to help her draft a letter to the pope pleading for the lives of the conversos. But Paul IV would not be dissuaded and went ahead with his murderous plan.

Twenty-four of the conversos, including one woman, were brutally bound, strung up, and executed by fire in a public massacre in the town square. The remaining conversos were commanded to stay in prison for the time being.

The horror of the pope's actions galvanized Gracia into taking drastic action. After meeting with rabbis and leaders of Ancona's Jewish community, she came up with a very daring but practical solution.

She would take a stand. A very brave and risky stand.

As head of the vast Mendes enterprises, Gracia controlled all its maritime activities in the port of Ancona. As step one in her strategy, she immediately used her influence to ban Mendes ships from entry into the port. This move, coupled with the actions of Jewish merchants who diverted cargo away from the once prosperous hub, brought business to a standstill.

Sadly, several months after it began, the courageous boycott backfired when the port was abruptly closed and abandoned. This resulted in a tremendous loss of revenue for the merchants and, more importantly, for the papal purses.

While the boycott was in effect, there had been strong opposition from Ancona's city council. Its members had sent an irate letter to the pope demanding that he banish the Inquisition from their city because it was antagonizing the eastern merchants and adversely affecting commerce.

Even though her embargo ultimately failed, no one could fault Gracia for not trying. She took great comfort in the fact that the seventy-two conversos who were still imprisoned were set free.

Word about Gracia's savvy strategy and incredibly bold actions quickly spread in Jewish communities throughout Europe. Hundreds of voices were now praising her daring and determination.

Most importantly, and amazingly for the time and place, was that it was a *woman* whose courage and moral outrage impacted the course of Jewish history. A renowned Jewish poet celebrated Gracia's actions, calling her "the heart of the Jewish people."

To this day, the exciting events she set in motion remain an inspirational moment in Jewish history. The year 1555 was recorded in Ancona as the date of the Jewish massacre, but it is now recognized as the time when Jews refused to convert to Christianity – and survived.

EIGHT

TIBERIAS – A DREAM THAT SLIPPED AWAY

F rom her home in Constantinople, Gracia became an important leader of Sephardic Jews throughout the Ottoman Empire. These people would eventually become the largest sixteenth-century Jewish community in the world.

But Gracia's heroic efforts were being made more and more difficult by the never-ending assaults on conversos. Their prospects of survival in the Catholic world of the Inquisition were growing dimmer and dimmer.

Gracia's deepest wish was to ensure permanent safety for all displaced Jews by giving them an alternative: settling in the land of their ancestors, from which they had been exiled for thousands of years.

Eventually, it seemed that her dream of developing a special area in the Holy Land for her people was becoming a reality. It would be in the ancient city of Tiberias, where, years earlier, her foresight had prompted her to lease land from the sultan.

Gracia put her son-in-law Joseph in charge of making her dream come true. By now an internationally recognized business leader, he had recently been named to the important position of duke of the Greek island of Naxos for his services to the sultan's court.

With Joseph's supervision, the crumbling walls of the site in Tiberias were being rebuilt and plans set in motion to construct homes for future Jewish settlers. Mulberry trees were planted in hopes of developing a silk factory as a spur to economic growth, and sheep were imported to establish a textile industry – all on Gracia's orders.

Tragically, despite the best of intentions on everyone's part, Gracia's dream eventually had to be abandoned. Reasons for the failure are sketchy in historical records. We can guess that she must have been heartbroken when her vision of hundreds of conversos and other Jews settling in their biblical and spiritual home disappeared.

But Gracia was no stranger to disappointment. She had often taken risks throughout her life and had consequently been put in extremely vulnerable situations. She found ways to cope time and time again. As well, Francisco demonstrated his wholehearted belief in her abilities when he took the extremely unusual step, for a man of his time, of bequeathing his share in the colossal Mendes enterprises to his wife.

That kind of approval helped transform Gracia into one of the most powerful businesswomen of her time by the age of thirty. By then, she too believed in herself and was certain that she could deal with any crisis, no matter how challenging.

Maybe that's why she was brave enough to tackle massive projects that others would never consider – even projects that could prove to be impossible, such as developing a major resettlement in the Holy Land, which at the time was largely an uninhabited sand-swept desert.

NINE

HOME AT LAST

Despite disappointments, Gracia had arrived at a new, blissfully peaceful and richly deserved time in her life. At last, her secret identity revealed, she was content just being with her family, friends, and guests. In the last decade of her life, she was rarely seen outside her home.

Anyone passing by her estate would likely have heard sounds of music, roars of laughter, and loud squeals drifting out the ornate windows. Those who were lucky enough to be invited indoors might have been surprised to find Gracia crouched in a dark corner motioning for silence. They might then have heard her whisper, "Please be quiet. We're playing a game of hide and seek, and some of my friend's children are trying to find me."

What she might have said next is a perfect metaphor for her daring and once dangerous life. "I am very familiar with the original model for this game. I used to play it nearly every day, wherever I went. But back then, it was never really a game.

"Hide and seek was the story line of my life and also the lives of many endangered secret Jews. It wasn't a fun game through those many years. It was scary. But that's what we had to do to survive."

TEN

THE GRACIA EFFECT

After Doña Gracia's death in 1569, Sephardic Jews continued to search in different parts of the world for a life free of persecution. Many settled in Holland, where they established a strong Jewish presence as merchants and traders, using skills they had acquired while living in Antwerp.

Seeking stability, others went to England, France, Italy, and North Africa. Meanwhile, the more adventurous braved the stormy seas of the Atlantic to reach the New World in the Americas.

Today, five centuries later, two countries are now trying to right the tragic wrongs of the past. Spain and Portugal recently decided to revisit their countries' historical narratives. Glaringly obvious was the brutal persecution of Jews, who were forced to convert to Catholicism and then flee Spain and Portugal without the right to return.

The result of this gigantic rethinking process was a decision to make amends by offering citizenship to anyone who can prove his or her Jewish origins.

Searching for evidence so far back in history might prove to be an impossibility. But an amazing discovery developed by British and Spanish scientists recently revealed, beyond a doubt, that the DNA of 20 percent of men in Spain today has distinctive Spanish-Jewish roots.

The striking irony in all this is that the Spanish and Portuguese governments are now seeking out the descendants of people whom their predecessors chose to persecute.

Doña Gracia Mendes is not a made-up character in a book or a movie. She is not a diva in an Italian opera. She was a very real person who lived five hundred years ago. If her life story seems almost too incredible to be true, that's because she was such an extraordinary woman – and her actions were so exceptionally courageous.

Dona Gracia was a remarkable woman for her time and was honored as such by those whose lives she inspired – secretly in her lifetime and jubilantly today. She was also the living embodiment of this famous quotation attributed to Theodor Herzl, the renowned visionary who is known as the spiritual father of Israel: "If you will it, it is no dream."

In Judaism, the expression *tikkun olam* teaches that our primary purpose on earth is "repairing the world." Whether Gracia was familiar with this concept is unknown. What *is* certain is that while living through the painful realities of sixteenth-century Jewish life in Europe, she tried mightily to repair the tremendous damage inflicted by sadistic popes on thousands of secret Jews.

Gracia died at the age of fifty-nine. Her gravesite remains unknown. But for a long time, it was believed that she was buried behind the synagogue that still bears her name today – La Senora in Izmir, Turkey.

Eulogies at the time called Gracia "a noble princess" and compared her to biblical heroes such as Yael, Deborah, and Judith. But we must not forget that the only weapon she used in her struggles was herself.

Sadly, the vast Mendes wealth dwindled after her death, as did the scale of its business activities – steadily siphoned off by creditors and bad investments as well as bribes and other funds necessitated by supporting an escape network.

It took a woman as phenomenal as Doña Gracia to steer her own course through the murky waterways of Europe on her own sail, all the while managing to keep the spirit of Judaism alive.

Today, visitors to Tiberias in Israel can trace this remarkable hero's life story at the Doña Gracia Museum, which spotlights her immeasurable contributions to the Jewish people and their history.

The feminist herstory movement is changing the records of Jewish history in many ways. Today, over five hundred years after her birth, Doña Gracia is getting the recognition she so rightly deserves in many ways. Among them are:

- Doña Gracia Day has been celebrated on her birthday (June 6) in New York and Philadelphia for more than a decade.
- In 2010, Israel's Education Ministry celebrated the five hundredth anniversary of her birth by introducing a Doña Gracia unit into the national school system.
- Also in 2010, the late president of Israel, Shimon Peres, gave her the highest tribute when he called her "a Zionist before her time."

Doña Gracia Mendes Nasi was an astounding original who is finally being recognized as one of history's most admirable Jewish heroes.

ACKNOWLEDGMENTS

I would like to acknowledge first and foremost my Canadian editor Terry Poulton, who was my critical eye and kept me going through many days and sleepless nights, and my editor at Gefen Publishing House in Jerusalem, Kezia Raffel Pride, who dazzled me with high-tech editing skills.

Thanks to my daughter Lisa, whose researching skills were invaluable.

Many thanks to Professor Laura Wiseman, Koschitzky Family Chair in Jewish Teacher Education, York University, Toronto; Professor Karen Krasny, Faculty of Education, York University, Toronto; Rabbi Miriam Margles, Danforth Jewish Circle, Toronto; Adina Moryosef, Institute for Sefardi and Anousim Studies, Netanya, Israel; Irit Achdut, Curator, Dona Gracia Museum, Tiberias, Israel; Simona Benyamini, Director, Bernard H. and Miriam Oster Visual Documentation Center of the Museum of the Jewish People at Beit Hatfutsot, Tel Aviv, Israel; author Giora Barak, Tel Aviv, Israel; Herbert Bishko, Tel Aviv, Israel; Greta Rosen, Ir Yamim, Israel; and Dr. Donald and Sharon Silverberg, Netanya, Israel.

BIBLIOGRAPHY

This book's contents are based on ancient and modern historical records including the following:

Birnbaum, Maríanna D. *The Long Journey of Gracia Mendes*. Budapest: Central European University Press, 2003.

Brooks, Andrée Aelion. *The Woman Who Defied Kings: The Life and Times of Doña Gracia Nasi – A Jewish Leader during the Renaissance*. Reprint, Vadnais Heights, MN: Paragon House, 2002.

Sloan, Dolores. *The Sephardic Jews of Spain and Portugal: Survival of an Imperiled Culture in the Fifteenth and Sixteenth Centuries*. Jefferson, NC: McFarland Books, 2009.

Roth, Cecil. *Doña Gracia of the House of Nasi*. Reprint, Philadelphia: Jewish Publication Society, 2009.

ABOUT THE AUTHOR

Marilyn Froggatt, author of *Doña Gracia's Secret*, coauthored, with journalist Lorraine Hunter, *Pricetag: Canadian Women and the Stress of Success* in 1980, when successful women were beginning to make their voices heard in the workplace, sometimes at great personal expense.

Marilyn earned a bachelor's degree in English from the University of Toronto. Later, while studying for her master's degree in Jewish studies at the Hebrew University in Jerusalem, she discovered Doña Gracia's heroic story. It went beyond words and into her heart, where it stayed for years. Telling it became her passion.

Marilyn lived in Israel for over ten years. While there, she produced short documentaries for the English-language television station.

She currently lives in Toronto with her daughter, son-in-law, and three grandchildren.